picnics

Hilary Heminway
& Alex Heminway

Photographs by Audrey Hall

Gibbs Smith, Publisher
TO ENRICH AND INSPIRE HUMANKIND

Salt Lake City | Charleston | Santa Fe | Santa Barbara

First Edition
11 10 09 08 07   5 4 3 2 1

Published by
Gibbs Smith, Publisher
PO Box 667
Layton, Utah 84041

Orders: 1.800.835.4993
www.gibbs-smith.com

Designed by Adrienne Pollard
Printed and bound in China

Library of Congress Cataloging-in-Publication Data

Heminway, Hilary.
  Picnics / Hilary Heminway, Alex Heminway ; illustrations by Hilary Heminway ;
  photographs by Audrey Hall. — 1st ed.
    p. cm.
  ISBN-13: 978-1-4236-0143-2
  ISBN-10: 1-4236-0143-2
  1. Outdoor cookery. 2. Picnicking. 3. Menus. I. Heminway, Alex. II.
Title.

TX823.H422 2007
641.5'78—dc22

2006026911

To Lucia Realini —

matchless cook, friend, and teacher

In Memory of Luke Puckett —

master chef and loyal friend

Contents

ACKNOWLEDGMENTS

We would like to thank the following people in no particular order (you're all at the top of the list): Audrey Hall for her photographs and steady friendship; Adrienne Pollard for her expert design; Gibbs Smith, Suzanne Taylor, Aimee Stoddard, Laura Ayrey, and everyone in Layton who built this book.

Thank you to greathearted friends: Pam and Fred Rentschler for their backyard and endless generosity; cuisiniers Angie and Luke Puckett; chef Tanner Raban; Pam and Michael Duffy and "deer" Annie; Stephanie Sandston at Shack Up; Dale Sexton, master of guide boat and grill; Troy Hyde and Julie Cox for a roaring good time; Kate and Harley Davidson; colorful Clyde Aspervig and Carol Guzman; "basket" cases Rob Richins and Judy Lentz; J&L Foote Associates for their wings; Jim Ellison and his well-mannered mounts; and hotrods Ralph Kenyon and Ronny Brunelle.

Thank you also to Rich Krevolin and Shana Smith, Mark Pesa, Gigi Aelbers and Ian Kellet, Ron Adams, and everyone at Yellowstone Jet Center. Thank you, Eileen Ehernberger and Debra Chase. Thanks to Chris Dabney's appetite, and Bruce Gillian.

Mighty thanks and love to Annabel and Clint Davis (Templeton Pug, too), to Parker Shipp, to Erin Goff for her wide smile, to Susan Pauli, to Sam Cofone and Billy Romanski at Sandy's, and to Priscilla Welles.

Thank you always to Kathy Niles, Jean Caswell, Harriet Vaughan, Sandy Johnston, Rhea Smart, and Pat Brownlee for their strength and support.

"My very photogenic mother died in a freak accident (picnic, lightning) when I was three."

— VLADIMIR NABOKOV, *Lolita*

"Carl would come every day to the park at the same time. And it was understood that I would give him lunch. I started making more and more elaborate lunches until they began to be full-blown picnics. I was aware that he was married. I was also aware of his reputation. I thought . . . I thought that as long as nothing progressed beyond the park bench, we were fine. And, for a long time, it didn't."

— ANITA SHREVE, *A Wedding in December*

Why Picnic? Dragonflies.

DOOMED, A PAINTED SKIMMER CUTS (cuts a hundred bias lines a minute) air rich with midges; curves past blue dashers (out for midges, too); breaks through pickerel weeds; stops short on a nodding monocot: a rush for rest. The dragonfly gathers across its sixty-thousand unit-eyes midge movement, leaf mass, eclipse. Frog—crops thorax, wings. Fell water sinks crux and quarry back again.

In other words, if you accept this carnal testimony, lunch delectated on the bank offers a wide view of the Pond (with a capital "P"). It's a whirlabout: force and surrender, vertex and mud. Don't be fooled by a sounding line's short measure: the pond is deep. Groups swim in circles. Everyone looks for food. Even bottom millimeters fill with fuss. Higher up, turtle is surviving right: that snapper has been basking two hundred million years in its carapace. Some sunbath.

Day to day we're outside to and fro, but rarely outdoors (if such a distinction can be made), almost never out-of-bounds. Too bad. Outdoors, green darners bend to green, bend to water. We might like to say, "They delight," but that would be personification.

In any event, *we* delight, bent to green, bent to water, should we bend at all. Unlike a Wunderkammer's lifeless mounts, the display on a pond's shelf stirs: bumblebee taps an inflorescence, whirligig gigs, frog jumps up and out on a golden section of circle. We stir to stir, so stir excites.

What is a greater argument for eating outdoors than the chance to see a frog swallow a dragonfly? None. Despite the sudden bites, harmony governs a pond. Its constituents know something about accord: turtles, frogs, and dragonflies have endured a ripple or two, the Cretaceous extinction for one. In *The Power of Limits,* architect György Doczi wrote, "By harmony we generally mean a fitting, orderly and pleasant joining of diversities, which in themselves may harbor many contrasts." That dragonfly was an expert flier but died in flight; it saw in all directions but couldn't see forward to the end. Take a short walk after lunch and, standing on the edge, you'll see direction coming.

— ALEX HEMINWAY

Picnics *for* One

BREAKFAST HOURS ARE WEALTHY HOURS.

Waking life is bread and quiet nourishment: a cup

of cheer, a bowl, a lone oriole sounding in the yew.

First light—to watch alone the growing luster on

the pond—is the first meal of the day. Last night's

coals are dim, so too the clamor of wine talk.

Spent glasses crowd the sink. Forget place settings, keep your Sèvres shut in

cupboards. Today's breakfast won't be a social gathering or a formality (the table waits

for later, busier productions, larger numbers, palaver). Leave the kitchen. In your

napkin, carry toast, jam, a knife. Outside under Norway spruce, nothing is the

matter. The weather report was a rumor. The progress of clouds, caught through

upswept branches, draws out the mind. Basking turtles, painted on rocks, teach

repose. Bees, fervid in mock orange, call us back to industry. The millstream, being

of a million parts of sound, delivers an irreproachable sermon: mind the water. So too

mind the earth and air. The footpath leads from kitchen door to public streets, but

not yet. The engine of our talk, stalled through dead of night, warms slowly.

What Becomes a Picnic Most

- Huckleberries, boysenberries, grapes

- Disregard for clocks

- Cradle of friends

- Cloth napkins

- Influence of clouds: arcs, tufts, flocks

- Water moving

- No money

- Lemon, lime, and vinegar (sour notes refresh in heat)

- Shade

- Atmospheric effects: light pillars, coronas, waves in the sun

- Buckeyes sipping nectar

- Expectations of night—*later, inside*

"Death is the sound of
distant thunder at a picnic."

— W.H. AUDEN, POET

Sunrise Picnic

Noah's Sunrise Coffee Cake*

Coffee or Fresh-Squeezed Juice

Newspaper

Our cousin Noah Emanuel, ten, wakes every visitor with coffee cake, his signature dish. Plate in hand, guests drift into the yard to sit under ficus or in the Hollywood sun. Breakfast is ideal for an impromptu picnic with quiet thoughts: Act III revisions, the day's pitch, strategies for beating traffic. Seasonal fruit is a welcome addition to this simple breakfast; it sweetens the guilt. Add coffee, tea, or fresh-squeezed juice in a thermos. Noah's cake keeps for several days (unless Noah is home) in or out of the refrigerator, and never crumbles.

Like Amalthaea's horn, your basket should fill with plenty.

NOAH'S SUNRISE COFFEE CAKE
Serves 10

THE PAN

3 tablespoons unsalted butter

1 tablespoon cinnamon

3 tablespoons sugar

2 tablespoons finely chopped pecans

Generously butter a 10-inch Bundt pan. Combine cinnamon and sugar in a small bowl. Dust pan with mixture. Sprinkle pecans into pan. Set aside.

THE CAKE

1 box organic yellow cake mix

1 box vanilla pudding mix

4 eggs, room temperature

1 cup sour cream

1/2 cup vegetable oil

1 teaspoon pure vanilla extract

1 teaspoon almond extract

1 tablespoon orange zest

8 tablespoons (1 stick) unsalted butter

1/2 cup sugar

1 tablespoon cinnamon

1 cup chopped pecans

1 tablespoon unsweetened cocoa

Preheat oven to 350 degrees. In a large bowl, whisk together cake and pudding mixes. Add eggs, sour cream, oil, vanilla extract, almond extract, and orange zest. Combine well.

In a small pot, melt butter. Add sugar, cinnamon, nuts, and cocoa. Mix until combined.

Pour half the cake batter into the pan. With a blunt knife, slowly marbleize (swirl in) half the butter mixture, taking care to keep away from the edge of the pan. Add remaining batter and once again marbleize with the butter mixture.

Bake 55 to 60 minutes, or until a cake tester comes out clean. Allow cake to cool completely before removing it from the pan. Serve.

At Your Desk

Seaweed Salad*

Sushi

Iced Green Tea

Fortune Cookie

Don't let the daily press—appointments, memos, calls—keep you from eating well. Food is purpose. We rise, dress, thread through loud crowds because we eat, and so we might. But the noontime meal is often savored quickly or not savored at all, an unfortunate attribute of our culture. If the pack is at your heels, take care, slow down, eat unopposed. They'll never catch you: they have nothing to eat. Seaweed salad paired with hand-cut rolls of sushi and a glass of iced green tea will inspirit you and your desk.

Strengthen your heart:
Gyokuro ("jewel dew") is true
tea, healthy and green.

SEAWEED SALAD

Serves 1 (with leftovers)

1/4 pound wakame seaweed

1/2 teaspoon salt

1/2 English cucumber

4 tablespoons rice wine vinegar

3 tablespoons soy sauce

1 teaspoon sugar

1/2 teaspoon wasabi paste

Soak wakame in a large bowl of water until soft. Drain and set aside. Peel and julienne cucumber. Salt cucumber strips and set aside to drain for 20 minutes. In a cup, mix vinegar, soy sauce, sugar, and wasabi. Chop seaweed and combine with cucumber. Pour dressing over salad and toss well.

Wakame grows in shallow waters—
and grows and grows. An invasive
weed, perhaps, but a benevolent one:
its pigment fucoxanthin helps burn
fatty tissues.

On the Plane

5-Mile-High Ham and Cheese
Ciabatta Sandwich*

Cornichons

Kettle-Cooked Potato Chips

Molasses Cookies

Empire Apple Dipped in Cinnamon
Sugar

Air travel is burdensome enough. The loss of control (we aren't flying the plane) adds to the anxiety of being so far removed from our birthright Earth. Food is a comfort in times of distress. Take control of your lunch: picnic on the plane. Build a simple, classic sandwich from pure ingredients: crisp watercress, generous slices of Black Forest ham, Gruyère (a nutty, firm Swiss cheese), and fresh ciabatta. Ciabatta ("slipper" in Italian) is a broad flat bread with crisp crust made from wheat flour. Remember, others have to share the plane cabin, a confined environment to say the least. Out of respect to fellow travelers, avoid odiferous foods like onion, garlic, and tuna.

5 MILE-HIGH HAM AND CHEESE CIABATTA SANDWICH

Serves 1

2 slices ciabatta

Prepared horseradish

Dijon mustard to taste

2 slices Black Forest ham

1 slice Gruyère

2 sprigs watercress

Unsalted butter

On bottom slice of ciabatta, spread a sparing amount of horseradish, followed by mustard to taste. Arrange ham over bread and add Gruyère. Top with watercress and final slice of buttered bread.

Nothing is general about aviation with a hand-built sandwich in your carry-on.

Picnics *for* Two

ONE OFTEN STANDS ALONE IN RAIN,

confused or composed. Either way a single voice

avers—*I am*—unchallenged by scraps of sound: finches

in the catmint, a collective shout from games played

round another house, a channel buoy farther out. Fog

is heavy. A train whistle predicts the distant city.

Come away, it seems to say. But no, this orchard is solid ground, one apple in the basket. But the crowd is thin: dragonfly, damselfly, congress of bees. The actor plays to empty seats. Talk is spirited, but conversation? One sided. *I am*—it ravels out as a spent ball of string exhausted on the floor. Wake up, don't forget why you came here. Those finches—*toweeeowee*—come to mind, and variations: dandelions constellate; boletus broadcast spores (the wherefore of mushrooms is germination). At pond's edge, a brace of turtles share pride of place. They bask as much in each other's light as in the sun's. One often stands alone at night—but why do fireflies bio-luminesce? Two. *Two.*

In the Basket

- Salt and pepper

- Flatware, the lighter the better
  (perhaps a spork, a knork), never plastic

- Tin plates, tin cups

- Seeds of conversation

- Bandanas (the same number as heads)

- Tablecloth, an old bedspread, a Pendleton blanket

- Pillows (transportation permitting)

- Corkscrew to open dandelion wine

- Binoculars

- Bear bells

- Backgammon, checkers, chess

- Relevant field guides

- Compass

- Matches, flashlight, candescent good cheer

The Sandwich

Gambling is heavy work. To sustain himself without folding, John Montagu (1718-92), fourth earl of Sandwich, first lord of the Admiralty, postmaster general, secretary of state, was rumored to have ordered (between hands) meat between bread; he never left his seat. But the sandwich has earlier antecedents. According to the Haggadah, Hillel the Elder, active during the reign of King Herod, wrapped Paschal lamb and bitter herbs in matzo. Although the modern variety is brittle, matzo of the first century BCE was probably soft, similar to the unleavened Armenian flatbread called lavash.

The selection of bread in any sandwich is of paramount concern; proportions are important: too thick, you lose the taste, too thin, you lose your lunch. The sandwich is the sine qua non of most picnics. "Sometimes the only thing for lunch is a great sandwich," writes Alice Waters in *Chez Panisse Café Cookbook*. She advocates using seasonal ingredients: raw scallions in spring, tomatoes in summer, sautéed kale in winter. But a perfect sandwich—the best ingredients well edited—is greater than the sum of its parts. It's an ingenious presentation, compact and portable, a small theater of big tastes.

Lakeside Picnic

**Hot Consommé and Sherry
in a Thermos**

Tuna Salad Sandwich*

Madeleines

Grapes

The tuna salad sandwich—friend to millions, foe to faint snuffers—is the preeminent American sandwich, second only to peanut butter and jelly. Although commonly encountered, it need not be ordinary. Fresh ingredients will ensure robust flavors. A rule of thumb when putting it all together: be provident with the mayonnaise; don't drown the fish.

TUNA SALAD SANDWICH
Serves 2

12 ounces white Albacore tuna in water, drained

1/4 cup mayonnaise to taste

2 tablespoons lemon juice

3 scallions, chopped

1 stalk celery, chopped

1 tablespoon capers

1 tablespoon chopped Italian parsley

Ground pepper to taste

Flake tuna with a fork. Mix all ingredients together and store in an airtight container. Prepare sandwiches at the picnic site to prevent them from becoming soggy.

Excellent additions to any tuna sandwich include romaine lettuce, watercress, thin slices of dill pickle, or thin slices of tomato.

Keep tuna fish light; it's a picnic cliché when abused by mayonnaise.

"Kissing a man with a beard is a lot like going to a picnic. You don't mind going through a little bush to get there!"

— MINNIE PEARL, COMEDIENNE

In Bed

**Grilled French-Cut Rib Lamb Chops
with Breadcrumb Garnish***

**Steamed Asparagus and
Baby Zucchini**

**Strawberries Dipped in
Balsamic Vinegar***

Breadsticks

How often do we look each other in the eye? Dinner alone at a private table, better yet in bed, is a greater gift than the restaurant redux, better than paint-the-town-red. It's less expensive, more romantic, and has fewer distractions, although different distractions attend.

GRILLED FRENCH-CUT LAMB CHOPS WITH BREADCRUMB GARNISH

Serves 2

THE BREADCRUMBS

1 tablespoon butter

1/4 cup breadcrumbs

1 clove garlic, minced (not to worry, both of you are eating garlic)

1/2 teaspoon finely chopped rosemary

1 teaspoon lemon zest

1 pinch kosher salt

Melt butter in a small saucepan. Add breadcrumbs, garlic, rosemary, lemon zest, and salt. Stir until golden. Take care not to burn the breadcrumbs.

THE LAMB CHOPS

4 French-cut loin chops

1 tablespoon extra-virgin olive oil

1 clove garlic, chopped

Breadcrumbs for garnish

In a deep dish, marinate chops in olive oil and garlic. Refrigerate for 2 hours.

Grill the meat over high heat for 2 to 3 minutes on each side. Remove from heat and garnish with breadcrumbs.

Feed each other by hand.

Fresh strawberries dipped in balsamic vinegar is a summer institution. The best strawberries are local and seasonal: Mohawks early, Northeasters mid-season, firm Winonas late. Balsamic is a dark, sweet Italian vinegar unique to the northern province of Modena. It has been made since the Middle Ages from the must of white trebbiano grapes. The highest quality balsamic, slow-aged from ten to twenty-five years, is labeled *tradizionale*. Since the 1980s balsamic has become ubiquitous in this country. It's best at the tip of a strawberry.

Serves 2

2 tablespoons chopped fresh mint

1/4 cup balsamic vinegar

10 organic strawberries

In a bowl, mix mint and vinegar. Dip strawberries in mixture. Eat with fingers.

Aerobic Picnics

THE HEART HAS A VERGE LIKE A HARVEST FIELD

hemmed with stones dug from its peculiar soil.

Every pitch has limitations: unhewn blocks, a stub–

born wall: protection and impediment. Along this

ligature lichen blooms and spreads, a slow course

of decay; all rocks in time weather and break.

Why wait until then to pass over the line? We're not bound, as a liege is, to strict

service and everyday ground. Quick, spring up from narrow furrows, run to the

fringe (it's no longer fringe when center of gravity follows)—a slip, a misstep or

two—foot finds purchase, then over wall to the other side. We've gained the forest

and clemency from the drowse of summer heat. The view here is one of deep

space: a mourning cloak sets a crooked course tree to tree until its black-and-yellow

wings beat elsewhere out of sight. The understory tells a vital plot: cinnamon fern,

royal fern, ostrich fern—that's just an introduction. What to eat on our first night

away from home? Mulberry, strawberry, apple. Small annunciations light this

larger room.

Who can deny the warmth of this
slow-burning stew? Ill humor and a
cold heart will simmer and reduce.

Snowshoe Picnic

Chilly Weather Chili*

Corn bread with Cheese and Chilis

Hot Chocolate*

One never outgrows the luxury of snow,
its swirl and whisper. We're hidden there
and remote. Snowshoes mark but briefly
the way we came. The soft crunch—
hear that?—is the only talk that matters.
A thermos of chili
carried up the mountain
and spooned into bowls reminds us of
the warmth we left below and steels us
against further cold.

Drink up (responsibly),
beer is liquid bread.

CHILLY WEATHER CHILI
Serves 8

4 tablespoons extra-virgin olive oil

3 pounds round or chuck, cut into 1/2-inch pieces

2 large Vidalia onions, chopped

1 fennel, white bulb only, chopped

4 cloves garlic, minced

1/2 jalapeño or more to taste, chopped

1/2 cup chili powder

1 teaspoon ground cinnamon

1/3 cup ground cumin

2 teaspoons oregano

1 teaspoon coriander

1/2 cup red table wine

16 ounces whole tomatoes, drained and chopped

3 cups tomato sauce

16 ounces black beans, drained

16 ounces kidney beans, drained

GARNISHES

Sour cream

Tomato salsa

Avocado

Cilantro

Chopped scallions

Tortilla strips

Shredded white cheddar cheese

Lime wedges

Preheat oven to 350 degrees. In a stew pot, heat oil over medium heat. Brown beef in batches. Remove beef to a bowl and set aside. Add more oil to pot if needed. Sauté onions and fennel until lightly brown. Add garlic and jalapeño. Cook uncovered for 1 minute. Return meat to pot. Add all spices. Stir continuously for 2 minutes. Add wine. Cook uncovered for 2 minutes. Add tomatoes, tomato sauce, and beans. Cover. Bake in oven for 45 minutes. Transfer to a widemouthed thermos. Garnish as desired.

Drink a mug of hot chocolate and peace is with you.

Vary the recipe (adults only) by adding a tablespoon of coffee liqueur and a cinnamon stick for Mexican hot chocolate, or a tablespoon of peppermint schnapps with a peppermint stick for a holiday cup.

A cup of canned heat beats back the despair of winter weather outside and in.

HOT CHOCOLATE

Serves 6

DRY INGREDIENTS

1/2 cup unsweetened cocoa

1/2 cup sugar

1/4 teaspoon nutmeg

1/2 teaspoon cinnamon

Pinch of salt

Combine ingredients in a bowl.

WET INGREDIENTS

8 tablespoons strong brewed coffee

1 quart milk

1/2 cup heavy cream

1 teaspoon pure vanilla extract

In a heavy saucepan, heat ingredients until just boiling. Remove from heat. Whisk in cocoa mixture from step one and beat until smooth and creamy. Reheat and bring to a boil again. Remove from heat and fill thermos.

Huzzah, the holiday!
A palliative sip is a
taste of glee.

"Great things are done when men and mountains meet.
They are not done by jostling in the street."

— WILLIAM BLAKE, POET

The Thermos

Fourth grade crept by, mostly under snow. Even after the thaw, the creek offered no trout. We christened sticks and leaves and floated them to battles around the bend. Spring ice knocked hard, sank many ships. Thermos empty, we stumped home, not marching anymore.

Use a narrow-top thermos for beverages, a wide-mouth for thicker mixtures.

- Chilly weather chili
- Split-pea soup
- Garganelli and ragù
- Fresh carrots in spring water
- Mulled cider
- Mulled wine

Goodness: Gorp

Offer gorp to guests in linen and they'll threaten to leave; trail mix is nutty under the gazebo. But pass it around the corniche and footsloggers will applaud. It's a perfect tonic for the trek: it's easy to carry and a ready supply of energizing protein (heart-healthy nuts) and carbohydrates. The etymology is uncertain; the word *gorp* may derive from the old English verb *gorp* (to eat greedily) or it may not. Regardless, it's good old raisins and peanuts.

1 cup mixed nuts (peanuts, cashews, almonds)

1 cup M&M's

1 cup diced dried fruits (apricots, apples, blueberries, cranberries)

1/2 cup raisins

1 cup sunflower kernels

In a ziplock bag, shake all ingredients. Breakfast cereal, granola, and chocolate chunks may be added, or substituted, according to preference.

Wilderness Backpack

Mystic Market Gourmet Granola*

Hardboiled Eggs

Dried Fruit

Crouched in an alpine meadow, a week away from home, we're among family nonetheless: aster, flax, showy fleabane. Air is thin; head is light from hunger and footwork. Granola is the ideal repast to fortify at high altitudes; it's lightweight, a ready source of energy, and can be transported in small containers or bags. Our favorite granola is made from organic ingredients at Mystic Market in Mystic, Connecticut, far from the Rockies but close in spirit to mountain meadows.

MYSTIC MARKET GOURMET GRANOLA

Yields 20 cups

THE BASE MIXTURE

8 cups oats

3 cups grated unsweetened coconut

1 1/2 cups bran

1 cup whole almonds

1 cup whole pecans

1 cup whole walnuts

Preheat oven to 325 degrees. In a large bowl, mix together all ingredients. Spread mixture in even, thin layers on several rimmed cookie sheets. Toast in oven for 10 minutes, or until golden brown.

THE BUTTER AND SUGAR

1 cup unsalted butter

1 cup dark brown sugar

3/4 cup honey

1 cup peanut butter

1 1/2 tablespoons cinnamon

1 teaspoon pure vanilla extract

Combine all ingredients in a saucepan. Bring to a slow simmer until mixture is thoroughly melted. Add in base mixture and combine well. Spread evenly on cookie sheets and bake again at 325 degrees for 12 minutes, or until crunchy and dark in color. Let cool. Break apart with your hands into a large bowl.

THE GRANOLA

1 cup raisins

1 cup dried cranberries or blueberries

1 1/2 cups banana chips

Add ingredients from steps one and two to granola. Serve. Granola can be stored in airtight containers for up to one month.

Picnics *for* Gathering Together

DRINK A DRAUGHT, THE LOT OF YOU, AND CELEBRATE AT ONCE;
FORTUNE, FITFUL HOST, CHANGES IN A STROKE.

Bell hammer hammers home each great or grievous

day, an even beat despite the unevenness to follow.

Gears and springs won't stop: black mantel clock,

wound tight, strikes, strikes—startles everyone.

What's happening? Clockwork. One day they'll come and pack away your toys,

grandfather's medal, the four-leaf clover found in backyard grass—even luck

gets tired. (Imagine that ancestral city where you might never get a chance to

walk: children on weekend streets; pretzels; beer; an oompah band on

the boulevard—it exists—a hill, a castle keep, ghosts inside who curse the brutal

duke.) Sunlight hammers whichever way we run. Rain too. This is serious—

lost charms, precipitation. A squall marshals on the lake. The boat is in a pitch,

but the oarlocks haven't rusted yet. It's time to row. Let's muster, drink a draught

together, and pull: we'll ask each other those questions we've been afraid to ask.

It's summer still, let's eat summer fruit.

Conveyance

A picnic is fellowship conveyed through food. Convey this message to your brother: let's pass from place to place together; the only heavy load is our fealty to the road and to each other. Don't worry, we have sturdy legs.

Most anything will suffice to carry bread from which to draw our strength.

- Champagne basket
- Backpack
- Cooler
- Suitcase
- Lunch pail
- Radio Flyer
- Paper bag
- Wheelbarrow
- Pockets
- Hands

Spaghetti Western (without the spaghetti)

Meatballs and Italian Sausage Skewers

Marinara Sauce for Dipping

Caprese Salad in Romaine Lettuce "Boats"*

Breadsticks

Figs and Gorgonzola

Although the Grotta Azzurra may be nowhere in sight, insalata caprese (in the style of Capri) is a fresh summer salad ideal for picnics. The best mozzarella, *di bufala campana*, is made from the milk of water buffalo bred in the Italian marshlands between Naples and Caserta. Campania's mozzarella, porcelain white, spongy, and rich in butterfat, is beyond compare when served within a day or two of its production.

Any ready surface serves a picnic: tailgate, bed, or driver's seat.

CAPRESE SALAD IN ROMAINE LETTUCE "BOATS"

Serves 6

I head romaine lettuce

I pound mozzarella, cubed

2 cups cherry tomatoes, cut in halves

1/2 cup chopped fresh basil

1/4 cup capers

1/4 cup pitted kalamata olives, chopped

2 to 3 tablespoons extra-virgin olive oil

Kosher salt and pepper to taste

Pull apart leaves of romaine head and wash. In a large bowl, mix all other ingredients. Fill leaves with salad. (The narrow obovate leaves of the romaine function as "boats.") For convenience, it may be best to assemble the salad at the picnic site.

Keeping Bugs Off

Insect repellents containing DEET are purported to be among the most effective on the market. The mainstream medical community recommends controlled use for the prevention of tick- and mosquito-borne maladies. Recently, pharmacologists found prolonged exposure to DEET causes diffuse brain cell death in rats. And it corrodes plastic. Forthwith, a list of holistic alternatives to N,N-diethyl-3-methylbenzamide:

- Stay home

- Eat a head of garlic (it also prevents thrombosis and vampires)

- Dab catnip oil behind the ears, but watch out for feral mousers

- Rub oil of lemon eucalyptus on exposed skin

- Employ bed netting to obstruct mosquitoes (and, sadly, the view)

- Burn citronella (candles or oil) made from Cymbopogon grasses

- Use pennyroyal to repel a dog's best friend

- Start a campfire

- Wear long pants and take comfort in an added benefit: they're more dignified than shorts

"I suppose I would still prefer to sit under a tree
     with a picnic basket rather than under a gas pump."

— ROY LICHTENSTEIN, ARTIST

Riverside Barbecue

Grilled Trout with Tartar Sauce*

Grilled Corn on the Cob with Citrus Butter*

Coleslaw with Horseradish

Blueberry Muffins

S'mores (graham crackers, toasted marshmallow, peanut butter, and chocolate)

Local production of food for local consumption is the battle cry of many chefs and gourmands; they lobby hard for a return to the cultivation of native varieties and to the art of gardening—hands in the soil, as it were. What could be more local than backyard corn and a creel full of rainbow trout caught under the cottonwood? Your hands are in the figurative soil: you've got to pick the corn and hook the fish.

GRILLED TROUT WITH TARTAR SAUCE

Serves 4 (if you catch 4)

THE TROUT

4 trout

Salt and pepper to taste

1 tablespoon chopped dill

1 tablespoon chopped Italian parsley

2 tablespoons melted butter

Juice of 1/2 lemon

1/4 cup olive oil

Clean trout. Salt and pepper inside and out. Stuff fish with dill, parsley, butter, and lemon juice. Brush skin of trout with oil. Cook until meat flakes when tested with a fork. The exact grilling time will depend on the size of the fish and the altitude at which you cook it (longer for bigger fish higher up).

THE TARTAR SAUCE

1 cup mayonnaise

2 tablespoons sour cream

1 tablespoon lime or lemon juice

1 clove garlic, minced

1 cup chopped basil or 1/2 cup chopped dill

4 dashes green Tabasco

Combine ingredients in a bowl and whisk together. Serve on the side.

Who wins the fight, antioxidant blueberries or butter in the batter? You win regardless.

Roasted marshmallows, a slab of chocolate, and peanut butter on Graham crackers—say no more, a s'more.

GRILLED CORN ON THE COB WITH CITRUS BUTTER

Serves 4

Break the cobs—Silver King, Silver Queen, Seneca Chief—from their stalks. Shuck, and boil. Listen to the mechanics of peck and return; the sound of summer is inside your head.

THE BUTTER

8 tablespoons (1 stick) unsalted butter, room temperature

1 tablespoon lime or lemon juice

1 teaspoon lime or lemon zest

2 dashes Tabasco

Kosher salt

In a bowl, beat butter and citrus juice until blended. Beat in citrus zest, Tabasco, and salt. Once blended, form into a roll and wrap in wax paper. Refrigerate or freeze until ready to use. Frozen butter can defrost en route to the picnic site.

THE CORN

4 ears fresh-picked corn in husks

When cooking corn over open coals, light coals 30 to 40 minutes prior to use. Wait until flames have subsided and coals are covered in a layer of white ash. Before grilling corn, peel away outer husks, leaving inner husks intact. Peel back, but don't remove, the inner husks. Remove corn silk. Rewrap ears with their inner husks. Grill corn, turning every few minutes, until husks are crisp and brown, approximately 8 to 10 minutes.

Catch and release are the watchwords, but who can deny the joy of purpose? To catch and keep is to eat.

Saddlebag Picnics

LAST APPLE GONE FROM THE SADDLEBAG,

gray mare clops down a steep declension, fords

Boulder Creek—the trailhead looms through spruce.

A hard-set line of base camps cramps the place.

Pinecones won't grow in dust, a truck-trafficked

acre. Goodbye lupine and panniered mules.

The transition is abrupt: a farrier hammers anvil in a nearby thicket; noonday fuss.

The basic facts—canvas, lanyards, rope—are folded, coiled, stacked. As we drive

back to the junction—stopping, starting at barbed-wire gates—old victors take

the field: whistlework, talk, dollars and cents: a hard-set fence. Tomorrow,

different campers will sit in today's saddle, crook up trails likewise to mountain

meadow, sweeten their coffee from our sugar sack. Fire will spit from a borrowed

brazier. Warmed, travelers will feel deeply the breadth of their presence. They'll

crow, "This is the key to life!" Traveler, a word of advice: remember well that

mountain meadow, lupine spilling from the woods. Don't break your promise

to those waves when anchored back at shore.

The Handy Kerchief:
Twelve Uses for a Cowboy Bandana

- Folded, a formal napkin

- Unfolded, a proper placemat

- Noontime hat

- Slim seat if not exactly a good cushion

- Cover for cherries in a sunstruck bowl

- Sandwich wrapper

- Plug for pinot when the cork is lost in grass

- Flyswatter (with apologies to Jains and their *jivas*)

- Rag to help clean summer soup from tin dishes

- Gag to stop the gab

- Plate in the absence of plates

- Trail marker—*Here I am*—an SOS flag

Sensibly Green

Time and again we spoil the woods, disrupt vegetation, leave trash, shout. This needn't be the norm. We can exert a green influence through consideration and self-control.

- Pack it in, pack it out. If not, your plastic champagne flute, ditched under the juniper, will biodegrade by the end of the millennium.

- The grizzly bear digs here. Give his muscle right-of-way. And the rutting buck on a hot date.

- Stay on designated trails. A tramp through undergrowth contributes to erosion and trail degradation—if the catwalk crumbles, you'll fall.

- Think of the common good: bury your dog's ordure, as well as your own, at least six inches under ground.

- It's safe to say Cascade won't improve aquatic life, although detergent lobbyists may carp. Clean your dishes away from fresh-water sources like streams and lakes (i.e., do them in your sink).

- If you must combust, build campfires at designated sites. Reuse existing fire rings. Burn only downed or decaying branches, not live wood. Never leave hot embers unattended.

- Save your spree for the nightclub; hullabaloo is out of place in the woods. It's nothing short of aggressive intrusion.

- Look at your reflection in still water. As vain as we are, we rarely see our true image. Who are we to ripple the lake?

"That faint semblance of Eden,
the picnic in the greenwood."

— HERMAN MELVILLE, AUTHOR

Trail Ride

**Turkey, Boursin, and Arugula
on Pumpernickel**

Wheat Montana 7-Grain Cookies*

Apples (for your health and your horse's)

Horses, like men, love grain. When snows drift shut the canyon and your steed grows thin, when you're enervated under hat, feed each other nutritious seven-grain cookies; they'll keep you both alive and kicking. These cookies are the specialty of Wheat Montana Bakeries in Three Forks, Montana.

WHEAT MONTANA 7-GRAIN COOKIES
Makes 4 dozen

**1 cup dried cranberries or
dried blueberries**

3 eggs, well beaten

1 teaspoon pure vanilla extract

1 cup unsalted butter

1 cup dark brown sugar

1 cup organic white sugar

2 1/2 cups natural white flour
(1 cup ground almond flour or ground
hazelnut flour can be substituted for
1 cup natural white flour)

1 teaspoon kosher salt

1 teaspoon ground cinnamon

2 teaspoons baking soda

2 cups 7-grain cereal

Combine cranberries with eggs and vanilla. Let stand 1 hour. Preheat oven to 350 degrees. Cream together butter and both sugars. Add flour, salt, cinnamon, and baking soda. Mix well. Blend in egg/berry mixture and 7-grain cereal. Dough should be stiff. Drop heaping teaspoons onto ungreased cookie sheet. Bake for 10 minutes or until lightly browned.

If you don't eat it,
your horse will.

A Day on the Hog

Biker Bread Salad*

Olives

Summer Sausage

Swiss Chocolate

No doubt this recipe ought to be among the many confidences (location of speed traps, houses of ill-repute) shared by high-waymen. Bread salad is best when carefully dressed: too much oil and vinegar leaves a mess.

BIKER BREAD SALAD
Serves 6

I pound haricots verts, trimmed and cut in halves

I fennel bulb, thinly sliced

14 cherry tomatoes, cut in halves

1/2 cup pitted kalamata olives, cut in halves

1/2 red onion, thinly sliced

4 ounces (1 block) herbed feta cheese, crumbled

1 clove garlic, minced

1/4 cup extra-virgin olive oil

1/4 cup red wine vinegar

Kosher salt and pepper to taste

2 cups rustic bread, cut in cubes

Steam green beans for 4 to 5 minutes, or until tender. Remove beans from heat and set in a bowl of ice water to prevent further cooking. Drain until dry. Add fennel, tomatoes, olives, onion, and feta. In a separate bowl, whisk together garlic, olive oil, vinegar, salt, and pepper. Pour over salad and toss by hand. To prevent sogginess, add bread 10 minutes before serving, no sooner.

Full disclosure: Biker Bread Salad is delicious but oxymoronic; offer salad to a biker and he may toss it.

Theme Picnics

A FLAME STARTS UP, KINGFISHER HOVER-HUNTING LOW MIDSTREAM.

Winds twitch, wings twitch. The river flickers

too in shallow places where stone and water

disagree. No, that doesn't sound right—it wheel-

spins over holding ground, a steady swing. Hard

by the bank, a painter at his easel can't compare.

His brush casts counterfeit light: fire fixed, sky a mess. He takes a different tack,

but tapered leader and hook won't lead to much. The loud sun has ransacked this

place. Vacancies open down the line. The crowd drifts elsewhere under

vegetated shelf, a narrow rest. Nothing there but filtered light, aquatic newt,

blur of goose. A crippled heft of wood persists, like a caravel wracked on a high

reef year to year won't budge. But lines and metaphor are vanity; wood is wood.

The scene here is pallid poplar downed, green continuance, and flood. An out-

break of caddis flies constellates above the glaze—a jump, a grab—every strike

is a golden try.

Do Your Level Best

- Pack it in, pack it out

- Gather seasonal fruit

- Eat with your hands

- Don't kill the ants

- Build campfires at designated sites

- Keep your dog from chasing wildlife

- Watch the common grackle

- Go out on a limb

- Spectate—it's thunder vs. lightning

- Lose your way

More than Mayonnaise

Although he didn't invent mayonnaise, Auguste Escoffier (august French chef) elevated the emulsion; in the early twentieth century, he pronounced mayonnaise one of six "mother sauces." It remains a steady presence in the kitchen.

A bowl of homemade mayonnaise is the perfect alternative to a jar of the heavy commercial type. Whisk egg yolks with olive oil, garlic, and a pinch of salt to make aioli, or with peanut oil, Dijon, and red wine vinegar for mustard mayonnaise.

If you seek something different for your sandwich, either unsalted butter or mustard alone is a straightforward solution. With apologies to Escoffier and his kitchen brigades, we include here a few alternatives, and simple changes, to classic mayo.

- Hummus
- Boursin herbed cheese
- Hollandaise
- Pesto alla Genovese
- Wasabi mayonnaise
- Chipotle mayonnaise
- Cream cheese
- Guacamole
- Tapenade
- Anchovy-garlic paste

" 'And this we do for pleasure,'
Greta McCraw muttered from the shadows,
'so that we may shortly be at the mercy
of venomous snakes and poisonous ants.' "

— JOAN LINDSAY, AUTHOR OF *PICNIC AT HANGING ROCK*

African Picnic

Tanzania Tomato Soup*

Cold Artichokes with Curried Mayonnaise

Chapati Bread and Hummus

Mangos

Ginger Snaps

Pass the mango, Bwana, pass the soup—armored crickets chirr in millet. Under moonlight the packed earth is candescent as old bone (not very) and hard. We feel chips and fractures under the milulu mat. The history of beauty begins here: an upright gait, tool making, speech. Three million five hundred thousand years ago, a family walked. Footprints divulge few facts—two adults and a child trailed through ash—but what fine facts. Look up, it's the same moon. Consider this: Tanzania is home.

TANZANIA TOMATO SOUP

Serves 6

4 cups V8 juice

2 cups tomato juice

Juice of 1 lemon

1 teaspoon lemon zest

3 tablespoons red wine vinegar

1 tablespoon curry powder

1/2 teaspoon Tabasco sauce

1/3 cup chopped fresh basil

1/3 cup chopped fresh mint

2 cups plain yogurt

In a food processor, combine all ingredients and blend well. Serve chilled.

Decant the noonday thermos; portable soup effects a portable meal.

Fit for a Queen: Tea Sandwiches

The traditional English tea sandwich—sliced cucumber between buttered bread—sustains during the hard stretch from teatime to dinner. Narrow and thin, or cut in small triangles, the tea sandwich is ideal for picnic transport. Serve these variations, crusts trimmed, on dense 1/4-inch brown bread:

- Red pepper jelly and cream cheese
- Boursin with small-seed cucumbers
- Gravlax, unsalted butter, minced dill
- Smoked turkey breast, basil, sun-dried tomatoes
- Watercress with mustard mayonnaise
- Roquefort and Granny Smith apples
- Sliced ham, unsalted butter, and horseradish
- Spring radishes, chives, chèvre

"Tea to the English is really a picnic indoors."

— ALICE WALKER, NOVELIST, POET

High Tea

Curried Egg Salad Sandwiches*

Cucumber and Boursin Sandwich

Oatmeal Shortbread*

The perfect meal is a rare accomplishment.

Ingredients are its meat and potatoes.
The simple curried egg salad sandwich,
made from eggs and daily bread, is a cele-
bration of our earthbound luck. Take
your sandwich out to the yard where few
meals are eaten. Let ants strike from the
flank, let birdcalls interrupt.

CURRIED EGG SALAD SANDWICHES

Serves 6

6 hardboiled eggs

1/3 cup mayonnaise

1/2 teaspoon curry powder (or to taste)

Salt and pepper to taste

12 slices thin white bread

1 heaping tablespoon chopped chives

Chop eggs. In a bowl, mash eggs with a fork. Stir in mayonnaise and curry powder. Add salt and pepper to taste. Using a biscuit cutter, cut bread into small round slices. Spread the bottom slices with egg salad. Dip sandwich edges in chives.

A tidy sum of tea sandwiches, crusts clipped, is a tidy meal.

Serves 4 to 6

Butter, sugar, flour, and salt are the principals of cooking. Although a simple combination, short-bread is a dense reward. It's best enjoyed during the hungry interlude between lunch and dinner when every earlier bite seems long ago and vague.

8 tablespoons (1 stick) unsalted butter, softened

1/3 cup firmly packed light brown sugar

3/4 cup flour

2 tablespoons ground almond flour

1/2 teaspoon salt

1 teaspoon cinnamon

2/3 cup old-fashioned rolled oats

Preheat oven to 350 degrees. In a bowl, cream butter with an electric mixer. Add brown sugar. Beat until light and fluffy.

In another bowl, whisk together flour, salt, and cinnamon. Combine flour and butter mixtures. Add oats and stir until just combined. Press mixture evenly into an un-greased 9-inch pie pan. Smooth top and prick all over with a fork. Bake in middle of oven for 40 minutes, or until golden. Remove from oven. While warm, score shortbread deeply with the edge or tine of a fork. Let cool completely in pan. Break into wedges and serve.

Backyard Formal

Shrimp and Morel Lemongrass Skewers with Mango Salsa*

Bison Tenderloin with Forrest Mushroom Sauce Served with Peruvian and Sweet Potatoes and Grilled Baby Summer Squash

Grilled Banana Bread, Vanilla Bean Ice Cream, and Caramelized Pineapples*

Pay for your picnic, hunt for morels (experienced mushroomers only). At upwards of $100 per pound retail, a carpet of Grade AA morels is a picnic indeed. Look under the ash, under the elm, in the backyard apple orchard. The springtime combination of sun, rain, and nutrients that prompts these porous ascocarps is an unknown sum. It's safe to say morels love soil disturbances, especially forest fires, and the nutrients released from decomposing trees. Celebrate the black morel—beware the false—eat them grilled on skewers, on toast, or alone on a plate.

Where are the morels? Back, back, behind that distant tree.

Generosity is an open hand offering an open plate.

SHRIMP AND MOREL LEMONGRASS SKEWERS WITH MANGO SALSA

Serves 4

THE SALSA

3 champagne mangos

I small red onion

3 radishes

I green bell pepper

I red bell pepper

I tablespoon honey

I clove garlic, minced

Dash of ground chipotle pepper

Salt and pepper

Peel mangos, cut flesh in strips, and dice. Finely dice onion, radishes, and peppers. Toss ingredients in a large bowl. Add honey, garlic, chipotle, salt, and pepper. Toss again, and set aside.

THE SKEWERS

12 medium-sized shrimp

I bunch lemongrass

12 fresh morels

I clove garlic, minced

Salt and pepper

Olive oil

Salsa

Peel and devein the shrimp. Remove lemongrass from its stalk. Peel outer layers and rinse well. Cut into four narrow 6-inch skewers. Skewer 3 shrimp and 3 mushrooms per lemongrass skewer, alternating shrimp with mushrooms. Season with garlic, salt, pepper, and a drizzle of olive oil. Grill skewers over high heat for 3 to 4 minutes on each side. Serve immediately with salsa.

Serves 4 to 6

In addition to math, bread making should be a required course for every high school student in this country. No loaf, no diploma. Unleavened bread, among the oldest prepared foods, dates to the end of the Stone Age, perhaps as early as ten millennia ago. Leavened dough rises later. Tortillas, pumpernickel, bò bîng, matzo—bread is culture. Bananas are elemental too; they bunched up around the same time.

1 pineapple

8 tablespoons (1 stick) butter

1 loaf fresh banana bread

1 tablespoon butter

1/2 cup brown sugar

1/8 cup dark rum

1 pint vanilla bean ice cream

Dash of cinnamon

Peel pineapple and remove core. Cut fruit in 1/2-inch-thick slices. Melt butter in a saucepan. Rub both sides of pineapple slices with melted butter. Over medium heat, grill until brown. Set aside to cool, then dice.

Cut banana bread in 1/2-inch thick slices. Brush one side of bread with butter. Grill buttered side for 2 minutes, or until brown.

In a large frying pan, melt 1 tablespoon of butter. Add brown sugar and stir until dissolved. Then add the pineapple and rum and sauté over medium heat until liquid reduces and thickens.

Serve banana bread with a heaping scoop of vanilla bean ice cream, topped with a spoonful of pineapple and a dash of cinnamon.

How can Man hate after eating banana bread and ice cream on a plate?

Plein Air Picnic

Stuffed Italian Chicken with Oven-Roasted
Tomatoes*

Orzo Salad with Peas and Yellow, Green,
and Red Peppers

Brownies with Chocolate Chips

Forza cucina Italiana! The Italians have
much to celebrate, and so do we: air-cured prosciutto
from Parma; fontina, a nutty-flavored cheese from
the Aosta Valley; triple-cream mascarpone, a specialty
of Lombardy, often used to thicken risotto but best
known for its star turn in tiramisu. Roll these ingredients together and your *cestino da picnic* will be
credited with virtue.

STUFFED ITALIAN CHICKEN WITH OVEN-
ROASTED TOMATOES
Serves 4

**2 whole boneless, skinless chicken breasts
(4 pieces)**

3 ounces mascarpone

3 ounces goat cheese (herb or plain)

1 tablespoon chopped Italian parsley

4 slices fontina cheese

4 slices prosciutto crudo

12 slices oven-roasted tomatoes (recipe follows)

12 basil leaves

1/4 cup flour

3 eggs beaten with 1 tablespoon cream

1 cup breadcrumbs

3 to 4 tablespoons olive oil

Preheat oven to 350 degrees. Pound chicken between
plastic wrap until thin. In a bowl, cream together mascarpone, goat cheese, and parsley. Spread along the
inside center of the chicken breasts. On top of the
cheese, stack 1 slice fontina, 1 slice ham, 3 slices tomato,
and 3 basil leaves. Roll chicken end to end, tucking under
the last edge. Tie in two places with kitchen twine.

Lightly dip chicken in flour, and then dip in egg batter. Roll
in breadcrumbs. In a frying pan, brown chicken bundles in
olive oil. In a baking pan, bake for 15 to 20 minutes. Serve
immediately, or let cool, slice, and serve the following day.

Hot-rolled or cold, stuffed Italian chicken is a compact dish, forceful and filling.

OVEN-ROASTED TOMATOES

Serves 4

Never mind the noxious members of the family— Angel's trumpet, Belladonna—they're pretty faces but bad from seed to stamen. The tomato (fr. Nahuatl *tomatl*) is entirely agreeable kin. The Americas can boast of many merits: Aztec plumbing, the airplane, and the tomato, our greatest indigenous berry. What would we do without it? No ketchup. No pizzazz. And spaghetti would be a nothing noodle. The heart loves a tomato. Critics and protesters, too: they see red and throw it.

6 to 8 tomatoes, cut in 3/4-inch slices

Olive oil

2 tablespoons chopped thyme

1/2 teaspoon sugar

2 tablespoons chopped garlic

Salt and pepper to taste

Preheat oven to 275 degrees. Lay tomato slices, cut side up, on an oiled cookie sheet. Drizzle with olive oil. Bake for 1 hour.

In a bowl, mix thyme, sugar, and garlic. Remove tomatoes from oven and sprinkle with thyme mixture. Add salt and pepper to taste. Return tomatoes to oven and bake for 1 more hour, or until slices are firm but not overly crisp.

Cold orzo salad served in its container is a
lucid lunch. Simplicity is a picnic maxim
Knotty preparation and fussy food distract
from blades of grass and bumblebee refrain.

Children's Picnics

IN LATE AUGUST, AT THE LIMIT OF ABUNDANCE, WE PICK SALEM
PEACHES AT LYMAN'S FARM.

The drive there—action, talk of peaches—gives

the children whet. To work for food, better yet to

grow it, prefaces the prize of eating. Soil is solace.

But soon it will be time to turn off heat and green.

The famished woodpile wants fattening for fall. We know what comes: the end of ripeness, sullen weather, and before it fear of change, that gaunt and hollow cold like a drupe's pitted core. Earth tilts. The hard etch of branches feels neither poignant nor cruel but bites nonetheless. Remember when it was summer and you were a child and you could lift anything: stones, logs, the couch by its leg. The ridge of a secret shell, chipped in a tumble, worried the hand—the only worry, except the time you knocked mother's china from its cupboard. Every day began with dash and tumble, a run from shell to shell. Light was everywhere, the lodestar in your pocket. Do you remember juice wrung from plums? Do you remember eating peaches in the woods?

Peanut Butter and . . .

- Currant jelly, old friend

- Local honey instead

- Sliced bananas

- Maine blueberry spread

- Garden lettuce, red onion

- Crisp bacon, still hot

- Golden Delicious, Gala, McCoun

- Dill pickles, believe it or not

- Carrots and celery, of course

- Fennel, an umbelliferae of sorts

- Mayhaw jelly, take it from the top!

- Durkee-Mower's Marshmallow Fluff

- Jalapeños, habaneros? Stop.

- Peanut butter itself is enough

Lemonade

Lemonade alone makes a picnic. A picnic without lemonade is a meal without. In 1676, the Compagnie de Limonadiers secured sole rights to dispense honeyed lemon water to Parisians. Louis XIV must have had a vendor's cup, although he rarely condescended to streets. In the twelfth century, Saladin's physician wrote a treatise on the lemon, so perhaps his sultan drank a restorative sip before putting the squeeze on crusaders. Horticulturists believe the lemon tree was originally cultivated on India's Deccan Plateau. Nearby is Sugriva's Cave, where Prince Rama and Hanuman first met.

Imagine those two up at night, the avatar and his warrior monkey, full of wisdom, valor, and citrus.

LEMONADE
Makes 1 generous quart

The slight bitterness of cucumber slices adds to the sour of lemons and the sweet sugar to make this a more complex glass.

1 cup freshly squeezed lemon juice (4 to 5 lemons)

3/4 cup fine sugar

4 cups water

1 lemon, sliced in rounds

1/2 cucumber, sliced in rounds

In a large pitcher, combine lemon juice, sugar, and water. Stir vigorously until sugar dissolves. Chill, add garnish rounds, and serve over ice.

"Hey, Boo Boo,
    what do you think is in that pic-a-nic basket?"

— YOGI BEAR

Caution: Causes Severe Inflammation

Poison ivy at one time or another has impugned every child's outdoor revels. Summer is a sham, it asserts. Pack up the fun.

In 1609, new to the New World, Captain John Smith (swashbuckler) observed of our indigenous treasure: "caused itchynge, and lastly, blisters." He named it "poison," an apt epithet.

Bedeviled, man has a habit of personifying what he can't understand—nature, numen—so he confers on this plant an evil mien: it trespasses as a vine, lies like ground cover, creeps when a trailing shrub, mimics tree limbs. Be warned, its compound leaves (three leaflets each) are mercurial: large, small, shiny, dull, ovate, notched. Nothing is certain but a bad rash.

Although poison, ivy it's not. *Toxicodendron radicans* is a member of the same family as mangos and cashews. Like its grievous siblings, poison oak and poison sumac, *T. radicans* produces urushiol, a toxic resin responsible for severe allergic contact dermatitis. A fortunate few are impervious: bobwhite quail eat the berries, deer nuzzle its leaves. Urushiol remains stable in dead or dried plants and may linger in unwashed clothes. Generally it will not spread on the body after it binds with skin cell membranes, fifteen or twenty minutes after contact.

Be sure to wash exposed skin thoroughly with both soap and water. Urushiol is hydrophobic: it repels H2O alone. Products like Tecnu and Zanfel are effective treatments that remove the offending oil. Cold compresses, calamine, antihistamines, and hydrocortisone are commonly used to relieve symptoms of the rash, which can last from one to two weeks, longer in severe cases.

The best solution is avoidance. "Leaves of three, let it be." If not—swelling, streaking, papules—summer promises more of John Smith's historic blisters.

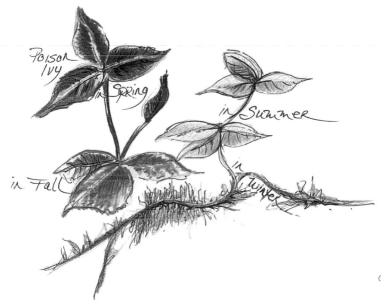

"When having difficulty sleeping,
rather than count sheep,
try to remember all the picnics you've been on."

— MRS. HOUGHTON P. METCALF, DOYENNE

Mesolithic man farmed little, scavenged often. Hand-to-mouth was not so long ago. Remind children of their ancestry: let them hunt for berries, apples, nuts.

Wildlife Birthday Party

Carrot Cake Sprinkled with Sunflower Seeds

Chocolate "Scat" Cookies*

Peanuts in the Shell

Iced Chamomile Tea

The chemistry of raising children is complex: cookies distract, but sugar excites. Childhood, however, is governed by a meaner science: goblins *do* live in closets. Regardless the adversary—sucrose or ghost— a cup of chamomile tea will relax. "Tea" is a misnomer. Brewed chamomile is a tisane, an herbal infusion made from the dried leaves and flowers of the German chamomile plant, a member of the sun-flower family, and not the leaves of the tea bush. As such it's not only caffeine free but also a mild seda-tive. Peter Rabbit, after much exertion, drank it down. It dispelled before bed the fear of being baked into Mrs. McGregor's pie.

CHOCOLATE "SCAT" COOKIES
Makes 1 dozen

4 squares unsweetened chocolate

1 can sweetened condensed milk

**1/2 pound whole pecans, toasted
then halved**

Preheat oven to 350 degrees. Melt chocolate
and milk in a saucepan over low heat.
Add nuts. Drop heaping tablespoonfuls on
a buttered cookie sheet. Bake until set, about
8 to 10 minutes.

How to describe these wicked cookies?
Suffice it to say, chocolate will banish
unspeakable thoughts.

What defines a picnic? It's a meal in
open air shared with brothers, paramour,
self—with all attendant in the woods.

In Case of Rain Picnics

RAIN FELL FOR THREE DAYS.

The wind blew all the petals off the prize roses.

Weather never fails. It may disappoint, but it never

fails. Monarchs in transit at end of summer—

Mexico so far away—buck and dip in updrafts

and downdrafts. But butterflies won't fail either.

Monarchs keep the circle—Canada to Michoacán—regardless of inclemency:

thunderstorms, hail, heat. Hind wings attract. Legs pollinate. Larvae are stout,

pupate. Adults grow fat in moist valley bottoms, fly north, south. Strong winds

are known to force them on an errant course. Frost may kill an unlucky colony,

two million caught in a treeless clearing. Regardless, the main, driven by the

implacable logic of migration, advances and returns. Great questions won't ever

be put to rest—How and Why—but elementary answers meet the test: tempera-

ture, milkweed. Bodies are stirred by weather, food, and rest. In other words,

celebrate the rain.

If It Rains

One minute the sun pushes hard, the next, a gathered scallop of
clouds ungathers. Head for cover: a ragtop, a gabled roof. Nothing
will be ruined. Eat your drumstick, drink your wet wine:

- Under barn's bowed ceiling

- Against the kitchen floor, it's a private park

- Within the close compass of an umbrella

- Around the hearth—fire is an ardent landscape

- On a screened porch

- Across the backseat—rain will stall

- In the drench where you are

"I've liked lots of people
until I went on a picnic jaunt with them."

— BESS TRUMAN, FIRST LADY

Rain Date

Watercress Soup*

Water Crackers with Herbed Butter

Baked Bacon-Wrapped Water Chestnuts

Watermelon Salad*

Be patient in the rain, it will pass. But we hope not too soon. Rain is music. Leaves are infirm, grass must rise. A bowl, like cupped hands, represents the primal need to give and to receive— fresh rainwater, the benefits of soup. Leaf vegetables are high in protein, dietary fiber, vitamins A and C, iron, calcium, and folic acid. Watercress is strength. Twenty-five hundred years ago, Xerxes fed it to his troops; they bridged the Hellespont and conquered Greece. Not for long. The Greeks ate watercress too.

WATERCRESS SOUP

Serves 6

2 bunches watercress

2 tablespoons unsalted butter

1/2 Vidalia onion, diced

3 cups chicken or vegetable broth

1/2 cup heavy cream

1/2 cup crème fraîche

2 tablespoons chopped mint

Salt and pepper to taste

Remove tough stems and chop watercress. Melt butter in a saucepan. Add onion and sauté until golden. Add watercress. Stir until slightly wilted. Add broth. Simmer 5 minutes. Remove from heat. Using a food processor, purée until smooth. Return to saucepan and add cream. Reheat over low flame, making certain soup doesn't boil. Ladle into warmed bowls. Spoon tablespoonful of crème fraîche into each bowl. Sprinkle with mint, salt, and pepper. Serve.

Fight water with water: eat watermelon in the rain.

WATERMELON SALAD

Serves 4 to 6

3 tablespoons lime juice

2 tablespoons fresh cilantro

2 tablespoons fresh basil

1/2 teaspoon fresh cumin

1/4 teaspoon chili powder

1/8 teaspoon cayenne pepper

1/2 teaspoon salt

4 cups cubed watermelon

In a large bowl, mix together all ingredients except watermelon. Add watermelon and toss. Chill and serve.

PICNIC SUPPLIES

Necessities
Baybreeze Interiors
25 Bay St.
Watch Hill, RI 02891
401.348.0722

Classic Picnic Supplies
7415 Meadowbrook Ave.
Brooklyn, OH 44144
216.749.1112
classicpicnicsupplies@yahoo.com

Duluth Pack
1610 W. Superior St.
Duluth, MN 55806
800.777.4439
www.duluthpack.com

L. L. Bean
Freeport, ME 04033
800.441.5713
(Canada and United States)
www.llbean.com

Orvis
Manchester, VT
www.orvis.com

Pacific Leisure
610 Cyprus St.
Pismo Beach, CA 93449
805.773.1952
www.pacificleisureshopping.com

Scully and Scully
504 Park Ave.
New York, NY 10022
212.755.2590
www.scullyandscully.com

Containers
Cigar Box
Cam Kirn
405 W. Boulder Rd.
McLeod, MT 59052
406.222.0841

Glad Bags
www.glad.com

Rubbermaid
www.rubbermaid.com

Tupperware
www.tupperware.com

Ziploc
www.ziploc.com

Natural Bug Repellents
Avon
www.avon.com

Burt's Bees Herbal Insect Repellent
www.herbalremedies.com

Buzz Away
Itch Nix Gel
www.quantumhealth.com

Mosquito Repellent Clothes
www.exofficio.com

Repel
www.repel.com

Dog Backpacks
Dog Scouts
www.dogscouts.com

PETCO
www.petco.com

Wolf Packs
www.wolfpacks.com

PICNIC FOODS

Catering
Mystic Market
63 William's Ave. East
Mystic, CT 06355
860.572.7992

Rocky Mountain Seafood
1940 W. Main St.
Bozeman, MT 59718
406.586.4930
bcline@bresnan.net

Sandy's Fine Food Emporium
15 Post Rd.
Westerly, RI 02891
401.596.2004

Susan Pauli
PO Box 582
Big Timber, MT 59011
406.932.4882

Breads
Le Pain Quotidien
New York, LA, Paris,
London, Italy
www.lepainquotidien.com

On the Rise
1007 W. Main St.
Bozeman, MT 59715
406.582.0272

Wheat Montana Farms and
Bakery
10778 Hwy. 287
Three Forks, MT 59752
800.535.2798
www.wheatmontana.com

Organic Freeze-Dried Food
Nature's Flavors
www.naturesflavors.com

Mary Jane's Farm
www.maryjanesfarm.org
1000 Wild Iris Ln.
Moscow, ID 83843
888.750.6004